BELIEVE IN YOURSELF

@ John Oller

Published By Robert Corbin

@ John Oller

Believe in Yourself: Mastering Confidence and

Self-esteem

All Right RESERVED

ISBN 978-87-94477-91-8

TABLE OF CONTENTS

Chapter 1 1

Work Of Wonder 1

Chapter 2 20

Recognizing And Challenging Negative Thoughts And Beliefs 20

Chapter 3 27

The Anatomy Of Inferiority Complex 27

Chapter 4 65

Entering Into A Discussion Can Be Nerve-Wracking, But There Are Several Steps You Can Take To Make The Process Easier: 65

Chapter 5 68

Revealing Your Truth 68

Chapter 6 90

Understanding Confidence And Self-Esteem 90

Chapter 7 95

Embrace Self-Acceptance 95

Chapter 8 99

Best Version Of Yourself 99

Chapter 9 106

Impact On Well-Being: 106

Chapter 10 110

How To Identify Your Positive Qualities And Gain A More Objective View Of Yourself 110

Chapter 11 116

Meeting Someone For The First Time Can Be Nerve-Wracking, But There Are Several Steps You Can Take To Make The Process Easier: 116

Chapter 12 118

Health And Everything Else. 118

Are You Happy With What You Have Co-Created? 118

Do You Want A Change? 118

Chapter 13 132

How To Start Your Morning 132

Chapter 14 137

The Mindset Of Confidence 137

Chapter 15 140

Cultivate Positive Self-Talk 140

Chapter 1

Work of Wonder

Develop a Positive Vision of Yourself

Close your eyes for five seconds… then open them so you can finish reading the book. Now go to the mirror. Now close your eyes for five seconds then open them.

What does your physical reflection present that your mental reflection is lacking? I am not talking about your height and weight or the pimple on your nose. I am talking about your inner person. When you close your eyes and think about yourself, are you Spiderman or Batman? Who are you when you close your eyes? Now, what happens when you open them?

Think of a time when you didn't have a belief in yourself and it held you back. Now think of someone you admirer – Close your eyes and think about how they would handle the situation.

What did you see someone else accomplish you couldn't accomplish yourself?

Self-Limitations

When you were born, you had no limitations. You had no idea what you could or couldn't achieve. You had no limits and you had over the top expectations. You had a superhero mentality. I remember running around the house with my brother and sisters and from all accounts we were superheroes. I recall... I was Spiderman, my brother Louie was Superman (he used a towel as a cape), and I forget whether it was my sister Kim or Sabrina who was Wonder Woman. We had no limits... no limitations.

There was a point in your life when you had a dream of what you wanted to accomplish and there was no stopping you.

Sometimes, I sit here wondering and asking myself, when did we learn limitations? When did it become easier to believe "I can't"? What happened to the belief of "I can" and "I will?" – Do you remember saying ~ "I dare you or anyone else to try and stop me from achieving my dreams." – What happened to your boldness? When did you stop believing in the plan God laid out for you? Did you ever know the plan? When did you start down this path of deception? And finally, who put your fire out?

In order to move forward, you have to unlearn the limits you placed on your ability to accomplish the perceived impossible. You must ask what it will take for you to regain your superhero mentality. If God laid out the plan, regardless of the path we took, as long as we resubmit to His instructions, we are directed back on course…. Right?

Isn't it funny now that you are thinking about it? It's funny because what you believe about yourself isn't true. All this time you have been wrapped up in your own deception about yourself. All this time, the doubt and inability to accomplish your dreams was limited from your own thoughts and beliefs about yourself.

The tricky part about knowing the plan created for you… is realizing there was a plan and there is still a plan in existence. Somehow we talked ourselves into working and believing our own plan. You put "THE PLAN" on the back burner.

Is there something you do every day which brings you joy? Is there something you do for someone else that brings you joy? I've found as we dig deeper into the plan for ourselves; you will find your plan always encompasses improving and pouring into the lives of others. I've found through the numerous counseling sessions I conducted the plan is rarely about self-fulfillment or self-gratification. It's about what we do for others. But it starts with a belief in you.

Self-Belief

It's time for your introduction. Yes, I want you to meet you for the very first time. To believe in yourself, you have to meet you where you stand then get to know you. If you met yourself for the first time, what would be your first impression? Now – stop – when you thought about yourself whose voice did you hear?

Remember, this is not about what other people say about you. It's time to find yourself and convince yourself that you are not all the negative things you believe yourself to be.

So let's start by introducing you to you. Self-belief starts with tapping into the positive characteristics which make up your 'YOU'; that make up who you are. Are you so beaten down you cannot find one nice thing to say about you?

Who is the person that co-signs on all your misery? I want you to listen to that voice (just for a minute). They said something nice about you at least once.

I am talking about the soothing ear person that is going to nod at everything you say; or the mental co-signer looking for a partner in misery.

If you don't have anyone to call, let's make a list of characteristics you feel you possess.

Remember, this is about mental development. In the HR world, we talk about having a 30 second elevator speech to describe you to a potential employer. Go ahead and do it. If you're in a public place reading this book, talk into your phone. We don't want folk thinking you're crazy.

Ready, set… go!

How hard was that? Were you able to positively talk about yourself for 30 seconds? Start thinking about some positive characteristics you expect to see in others. Do you see them in YOUrself… no really! Ask yourself the hard questions. – look at yourself to see if you have any of those characteristics. Think positive; with positive being the optimum word. You are renewing your mind… Here are some characteristics to consider:

I think quickly on my feet
I am educated (from books or the street)
I am charismatic
I am popular
I find it easy to talk to people

I have a positive attitude

I handle pressure situations

I have a sense of humor

I take constructive criticism

I give my time and talents

Yea, there are a lot of 'I's" in there. It's your list. As you're creating your list, really think about what each statement means to you and how effectively you execute each aspect of the sentence you read. Are you being realistic?

Next, take the list and jot down what you need to improve on in each of the characteristics you laid out.

For instance:

I handle situations well (after I calm down). That means you have to work on not blowing up.

I give my time and talents (but their meetings are too long and I don't like the leaders). You have to learn to work on other people's terms.

You are filled with many positive characteristics that have been suppressed or have gone unnoticed by you. So, how do you like you so far?

Self-Encouragement

And David was greatly distressed, for the people spoke of stoning him, because all the people were bitter in soul, each for his sons and daughters. But David strengthened himself in the Lord his God. Once you make up your mind to make positive deposits into YOUrself – you can be transformed into your positive view of YOUrself- ~ then you will need fewer deposits from peanut gallery to validate who you are. Ok... here is the tricky part.

In some aspects of religion and church, we depend on the pastors to be the motivational speaker in our lives and not just provide the spiritual guidance. The Praise and Worship team provides the theme music and not assist in setting the atmosphere. And the rest of the congregation becomes the judge and jury.

We all need a relevant Word from God.

When the naysayers came against David, he didn't wait until Sunday or Wednesday to be refueled; he encouraged and strengthened himself. Sometimes we have to be our own cheerleader.

Rah, Rah Me!

When you start your day with your theme music (we will discuss later in this chapter), rehearse your elevator speech, and then remember all the things you are capable of doing.

Inner Voice

If you read my last book Effective Leaders: Mentor *People and Manage Processes* – you see the discussion I have with my inner voice. My inner voice is inquisitive, encouraging, and straight to the point. My inner voice and I have a "love-love" relationship. It didn't always work that way. I use to hate the things I would say to myself; about myself. It took many soul searching journeys to take control of my inner voice. What type of verbal exchange do you have with your inner voice? Is that voice an ally or an enemy? By who, what, and when was your voice developed? Who shaped that voice? Whose voice do you hear in your mind when decisions are being made about your life?

Understand the voices you hear will come from various sources based on the experiences you had throughout your life. I've heard my grandma's voice, my Nanny, Papa Nick, my Mother, Father, sister and brothers, friends, enemies, pastors, teachers, and even strangers; I've heard voices from movies and sitcoms. Heck, I ain't ashamed to say I even heard bugs bunny and numerous cartoon characters from my childhood. These are the voices that shape your decisions and often time promote or limit your actions. These voices attempt to define you. However, if bugs bunny gives me advice, I have to think twice about the source... I must realize Bugs Bunny isn't always right   just saying

How often do you hear God's Voice; the voice from the knowledge of His Word? I aint getting preachy on you ~ But He said you are "fearfully and wonderfully made~ Wonderful are your works; my soul knows it very well.

Fearful Spirit

Have you ever done something out of fear or with a fearful spirit? You may think that means scared But fearfully in this context is out of perfection!

No mistakes, no excuses! You have been created with precision – it's time to release the thoughts that minimize who you are. ~ "Silly Rabbit, tricks are for Kids"~ When did these voices start to turn on you?

When you hear your inner voice, the first thing you need to do is look at the source. Is it in alignment and in direction of God's Word? If not, why are you giving that voice so much power over your actions? Where did the source get its power over you?

If my broke friend is giving me advice on finances. I must disregard the advice on money management but listen to how he mismanaged. If my single friend is giving me advice on my marriage, I may need to disregard some of the advice on making my marriage last but I may need to listen to the things that destroyed his marriage. If a dreamer is giving me advice on my vision… disregard!

Segmentation

Who and what makes up your inner voice? It's time for you to separate the voices that lead to your decisions and the perception you have of yourself! Focus on Y. O. U. not I.O.U. – You owe no one anything but you owe yourself everything.

Putting your inner voice into the proper segment is critical for improving how you feel about you. As I engage individuals in search of themselves, I have found most of them are battling with what others have said about them as opposed to what is in front of them; consider the source. Yes, you will hear consider the source over and over from me in this book; so, consider the source.

When the disciples told Jesus that folk was telling them various things about him - the only thing Jesus said was "who do you say I am?" Matthew As you consider the various sources which have forged your thinking about YOUrself how much weight do you give those thoughts? Are the thoughts negative or positive?

At My Worst

Have you heard this saying, I am my worst critic I am hard on myself Have you ever said this to yourself? Why are you so hard on yourself? What actions have you taken to improve upon the critiques? I didn't start believing in myself until I became my greatest cheerleader!

Once I realized the voices in my head weren't in the tone of my voice ~ I started the process of change. When I didn't just hear bugs bunny, nana, and them, and I started hearing my own voice; I started to change!

When you start criticizing yourself – what voice do you hear? Instead of saying I am my worst critic – become your greatest ally. Become the "can do" voice not the "won't do" voice. Leave the 'Debbie Downer's' of your life at the curb.

Most importantly, don't be a Downer to YOUrself. Find your inner voice; listen to your inner voice. Stop listening to respond and listen to comprehend. We have to deal with the inner me so you are able to face the outer me.

Attitude Adjustment

Do not conform to the pattern of this world, but be transformed by the renewing of your mind. One of my favorite sayings is "doing a check-up from the neck up." To adjust your attitude, we have to adjust our mind. Bishop Waylyn Hobbs Jr.'s Book "New Mind, New You" nails this biblical concept.

You have been created without a flaw; but know you are not perfect. The mind must be renewed and reconditioned to find your true self.

How do you recondition your mind after years and years of battering? After years and years of believing your self-worth aint what it ought to be? The simple answer...

Theme Music

Before every speech or presentation I give, I like to start with my theme song "Gonna Fly Now" the theme from the movie 'Rocky'. It's something about hearing the horns in the beginning of the song that gets the fire burning inside of me. Did you hear it in your mind – did you see the pictures of a man punching on beef and running up steps in Philadelphia come to my mind. Never staying down on the canvas, just getting back up! Overcoming!

What song do you play when you have stuff on your mind? When the voices are going off in your head condemning and torturing you? What songs are you listening to?

Saints... some of those songs you listen too about the testimony... well (in my church voice), if you focus on the testimony and not the overcoming. You are wallowing in the problem and not hearing the solution. Do you like the song because of the beginning and are you getting to the end? It's inspirational but you focus on the going through and not the fight through.

What is your theme song? The how you lost your love song... or the I am so alone song, don't count! What is your theme song? Is it triumphant?

Your theme song needs to focus on what is right about you. You have to walk away from that song with a self-belief and determination that will push you to want to improve who you are. Have you ever listened to a song that makes you want to run out the door and tackle the world?

Motivational Music

Listen to any motivational speaker and I am talking about some preachers. They walk up to the podium after a good motivational and inspirational rendition of something; then blow you away.

I know I should call this book the book of questions. You see, it's the unanswered or unasked questions that have you doubting yourself. The beautiful thing is all the questions will be at the back of the book. If you can answer them, you have transformed who you are.

Chapter 2

Recognizing and Challenging Negative Thoughts and Beliefs

As we just mentioned, you need to be able to recognize LSE and the self-beliefs that accompany it before you can begin to correct those negative ideas. The key to identifying low self-esteem lies in spotting behavior that shows evidence of the 4 basic psychological fears that were discussed in the last section.

Recognizing Negative Self Beliefs

Sometimes, people think so little of themselves that it is easy to spot low self-esteem. But a quick look at the fears and symptoms of a poor self image which we already covered show that sometimes identifying LSE can be difficult. It is not as clear-cut. For example, a confident acting person may always exhibit a high self-image, only because he is afraid that others will see what he believes is his truly inadequate self

The following behaviors and actions are often present in people with low self-esteem:

- A person expresses an "always or never" belief system.
- Someone constantly interrupts, attempts to finish your sentences and thoughts for you, and is always jumping to conclusions.
- The word "should" is constantly used. For instance, "I shouldn't have tried that" or "I should have accepted the job."
- A person makes huge generalizations based on little information or a single occurrence.
- Irrational behavior springs from emotional thinking that is not in line with factual information.

- A person often refers to himself as an "idiot", "failure" or "dummy".
- Someone tends to make everything personal, often blaming herself irrationally.
- Seeing every possible outcome as a catastrophe.
- Constantly seeking approval.
- Focusing on pain and pessimism.

The above behaviors and actions are common to people that have negative self-beliefs. Anxiety and depression, addiction and poor health are just a few of the symptoms of this type of mindset if it is allowed to exist over time, as we saw earlier. That is why it is so important to be able to recognize statements and actions that are symptomatic to a person suffering from .

Challenging Negative Thoughts

Once identified, harmful self-beliefs need to be challenged. Psychologists call any incorrect self-belief a "cognitive distortion". These are irrational and exaggerated ideas, beliefs and thoughts. Obviously, if someone suffers from cognitive distortion, their nonfactual beliefs could lead to behaviors and actions that deliver many of the negative consequences of LSE we discussed earlier.

One way to challenge cognitive distortion is to write out a cheat-sheet with LSE-challenging **statements**. Keep this list on you and refer to it often, especially when you recognize some of the symptoms of a poor self-image that we just covered. Challenge your negative and incorrect thoughts and beliefs with the following list of statements:

If you catch yourself saying **"I got lucky",** remind yourself that instead, you actually were prepared and worked really hard to reach some goal.

If you missed getting that big promotion, and you find yourself believing that you will never advance in your career, think this instead. Recognize this speed bump as a single negative event, but not who you are. Tell yourself that you will get the next promotion, and will work harder to make sure that happens.

If you catch yourself **constantly seeing negatives**, focus on the positive. Challenge your *"always negative"* beliefs by aggressively looking for positive, rewarding, uplifting and invigorating occurrences in your everyday life. When you spend time looking for positive events and thoughts, fewer negative thoughts enter your mind.

Are you constantly jumping to conclusions? A couple of minor failures happen in the morning, so you immediately think, "This is going to be the worst day ever!" This is a limiting belief that could create a self-fulfilling prophecy. Instead, think about the justification or conclusion you are making, and consider if it is rational or not.

Remember, if you use words and phrases like **"all of the time", "always" and "never",** you are practicing what psychologists call all-or-nothing thinking. Perhaps you think that you never get lucky. Challenge that mindset by identifying times when you truly did experience good fortune.

If you personalize everything, **assuming personal responsibility** for things outside of your control, you need to challenge that belief. If you are honest with yourself, and think logically, you will see that certain things cannot be controlled by you. Try to determine if you have true control over a particular outcome before you blame yourself for it.

Challenging negative and incorrect self-belief is critical if you are going to enjoy a rational "real world" view of yourself and society. **You are worthy of love, success, happiness and peace.** And you only need to continue recognizing limiting thoughts and challenging them with sensible ones to begin to reap the wonderful rewards that a healthy self-image delivers.

Chapter 3

The Anatomy of Inferiority Complex

Understanding the Concept:

This pivotal section of Chapter 1 delves into the heart of what an inferiority complex truly means. It's not merely a fleeting moment of self-doubt or a sporadic lack of confidence; rather, it's a profound and enduring sense of personal inadequacy that infiltrates every facet of an individual's life. Let's explore this concept further:

 Defining Inferiority Complex: The chapter opens with a clear and concise definition, setting the stage for readers to comprehend the core concept. An inferiority complex is a deep-seated belief that one is inherently flawed, insufficient, or less capable than others. It's a mental framework in which individuals habitually view themselves as inadequate in comparison to their peers and, as a result, perceive themselves as unworthy of success, happiness, or love.

Identifying Signs and Symptoms:

This section of Chapter 1 takes a closer look at the signs and symptoms of an inferiority complex, helping readers become more attuned to its presence, whether in themselves or others. Recognizing these indicators is a pivotal initial step in addressing the complex. Here's a deeper exploration:

Chronic Self-Criticism: Chronic self-criticism is often one of the most prominent indicators of an inferiority complex. It's an ongoing, negative internal dialogue where individuals constantly berate themselves. They focus on their flaws, real or perceived, and become their own harshest critics. This section helps readers identify if their self-talk is predominantly self-deprecating.

Avoidance of Challenges: Those with an inferiority complex may avoid taking on challenges or pursuing opportunities. Fear of failure or the belief that they're not capable of success can lead to a reluctance to step out of their comfort zones. Recognizing this avoidance behavior can be the key to understanding how the complex is impacting one's life.

Social Withdrawal: Social withdrawal is another significant symptom. Individuals with an inferiority complex may withdraw from social interactions and isolate themselves. They might feel unworthy of the company of others or fear judgment and rejection. By noticing their tendency to withdraw, readers can begin to address the complex's influence on their social life.

Constant Need for External Validation: People with an inferiority complex often seek external validation to compensate for their lack of self-worth. They rely on others' approval and praise to feel good about themselves. This section helps readers reflect on whether they have an excessive need for validation from others, which can be a sign of the complex.

Perfectionism: Perfectionism can be a symptom of an inferiority complex. Individuals may set impossibly high standards for themselves and become obsessed with flawlessness. When they inevitably fall short of these unrealistic expectations, it reinforces their feelings of inadequacy. Recognizing perfectionism is a key step toward understanding the complex's impact on personal and professional life.

By providing insight into these signs and symptoms, this section empowers readers to self-reflect and acknowledge if an inferiority complex is influencing their thoughts and behaviors. Additionally, it enables them to recognize these traits in others, which can be essential for offering support and understanding. Identifying these symptoms is the first step in addressing the complex and embarking on a journey of self-discovery and transformation.

3 Psychological Underpinnings:

This section delves into the deeper psychological mechanisms that contribute to the development and perpetuation of this complex, providing readers with insights into the intricate workings of the human mind. Let's delve into this in more detail:

Early Life Experiences: The psychological underpinnings often trace their roots to early life experiences. These experiences can include childhood traumas, consistent negative feedback, or an environment where success was hard to achieve. These early impressions can create a foundation for the development of an inferiority complex. It's vital to recognize that these experiences are not the fault of the individual, but they significantly shape their self-perception.

Social Comparison: The tendency to compare oneself with others is a significant psychological factor. People with an inferiority complex frequently engage in what psychologists call "social comparison." This is where they continually measure themselves against others, focusing on their shortcomings and minimizing their strengths. Understanding this mechanism is pivotal because it elucidates how your mind constantly put you at a disadvantage.

Negative Self-Talk: Negative self-talk plays a fundamental role. The inner dialogues within individuals with an inferiority complex are typically characterized by harsh self-criticism. They frequently berate themselves, emphasizing their perceived shortcomings. This section highlights how such negative self-talk reinforces feelings of inadequacy and affects self-esteem.

Cognitive Biases: Cognitive biases are systematic patterns of deviation from norm or rationality in judgment, often leading to perceptual distortion, inaccurate judgment, illogical interpretation, or what is broadly called irrationality. These biases are inherent to human cognition and can significantly impact decision-making and thought processes. In the context of an inferiority complex, understanding these biases is crucial, as they play a key role in reinforcing feelings of inadequacy. Here, we'll elaborate on some common cognitive biases:

Confirmation Bias: This bias refers to the tendency to search for, interpret, and remember information that confirms one's preexisting beliefs or values while ignoring or downplaying information that contradicts those beliefs. In the context of an inferiority complex, individuals may selectively focus on evidence that reinforces their negative self-perceptions and overlook or dismiss evidence that suggests otherwise. For example, if they receive praise for their work, they might attribute it to luck rather than their abilities.

Self-Serving Bias: The self-serving bias is the tendency to attribute positive events or outcomes to one's own character, while attributing negative events to external factors. In the context of an inferiority complex, individuals might attribute their successes to external factors or luck, diminishing their sense of accomplishment, while attributing their failures solely to their own shortcomings. This bias can perpetuate self-doubt and a lack of self-worth.

Dunning-Kruger Effect: The Dunning-Kruger effect is a cognitive bias in which individuals with low ability at a task tend to overestimate their ability, while those with high ability may underestimate their competence. In the context of an inferiority complex, individuals might erroneously believe they lack skills or knowledge, even when they possess them, due to their low self-esteem. This bias can lead to a lack of self-confidence and a persistent belief in their inadequacy.

Anchoring Bias: Anchoring bias occurs when individuals rely too heavily on the first piece of information encountered when making decisions. People with an inferiority complex may anchor themselves to negative self-beliefs formed early in life, which can significantly influence their self-perception and decision-making. For instance, if they were criticized or labeled as "unskilled" in their youth, they may continue to anchor their self-image to this negative assessment, even when evidence contradicts it.

Selective Perception: Selective perception involves perceiving and interpreting information in a way that aligns with preexisting beliefs and expectations. Individuals with an inferiority complex may selectively perceive feedback or comments from others, focusing on anything that reinforces their negative self-image while ignoring praise or encouragement.

Understanding these cognitive biases is vital, as they can perpetuate an inferiority complex by distorting one's self-perception and reinforcing self-doubt. Recognizing these biases is the first step in breaking free from their influence, fostering self-awareness, and embarking on a journey to build self-belief and healthier self-esteem. It's important to remember that cognitive biases are common to all individuals and do not reflect inherent deficiencies; they are products of how our minds naturally work.

Self-Fulfilling Prophecy: The psychological underpinnings also introduce the concept of self-fulfilling prophecies. People with an inferiority complex often believe they will fail or be rejected, and this belief can lead to behaviors that result in those outcomes. Recognizing this cycle is crucial, as it demonstrates how self-doubt can become a self-fulfilling prophecy, perpetuating the complex. By examining these psychological underpinnings, readers gain a deeper understanding of why an inferiority complex takes root and persists. They realize that it's not just a matter of lacking confidence; it's a complex interplay of early experiences, cognitive processes, and self-beliefs. Recognizing these psychological factors is the first step in breaking the cycle and embarking on a journey to heal and build self-belief.

The Importance of Awareness

Awareness is a fundamental aspect of human consciousness that plays a pivotal role in our daily lives and personal growth. It involves being in tune with ourselves, our surroundings, and the world at large. This heightened state of consciousness is vital in numerous aspects of life, from self-improvement to building better relationships and achieving personal and professional success.

Self-awareness:

Self-awareness is the foundation of personal growth and development. It involves understanding one's own emotions, thoughts, beliefs, and behaviors. When we are self-aware, we can identify our strengths and weaknesses, making it easier to set and achieve personal goals.

Self-awareness enables us to recognize and manage our emotions, which is a critical component of emotional intelligence. It allows us to respond rather than react impulsively, fostering better decision-making and healthier relationships

Understanding Emotions:Self-awareness includes recognizing and understanding one's own emotions. This means not only being aware of what you're feeling but also comprehending why you're feeling that way. This insight into your emotional landscape helps you manage your emotional responses more effectively.

Thoughts and Beliefs: Self-awareness extends to your thought patterns and belief systems. It involves an examination of your inner dialogue, the stories you tell yourself, and your core beliefs about yourself and the world. Understanding these cognitive processes can help you identify and change self-limiting beliefs and thought patterns.

Strengths and Weaknesses: Self-awareness involves acknowledging your strengths and weaknesses. Recognizing your strengths allows you to leverage them to your advantage. On the other hand, being aware of your weaknesses helps you take steps to improve or compensate for them.

Emotional Intelligence: Self-awareness is a fundamental component of emotional intelligence . By understanding your own emotions, you're better equipped to understand and empathize with the emotions of others. This leads to improved interpersonal relationships and more effective communication.

Response vs. Reaction: One of the key benefits of self-awareness is the ability to respond rather than react. Reacting is often impulsive and can lead to negative outcomes, while responding is a more considered and intentional action. Self-aware individuals can step back, evaluate a situation, and make more thoughtful decisions.

Healthy Relationships: When you're self-aware, you can communicate your needs, desires, and boundaries more clearly in your relationships. This contributes to healthier and more satisfying interactions with others, whether in personal or professional contexts.

In essence, self-awareness provides you with a greater sense of control over your thoughts, emotions, and behaviors. It allows you to make more conscious choices, set meaningful goals, and work toward personal growth. It's a powerful tool for improving not only your relationship with yourself but also your relationships with others and your overall quality of life.

Emotional intelligence:

Awareness of one's own emotions and the emotions of others is a central element of emotional intelligence. This awareness empowers us to empathize with others, communicate effectively, and resolve conflicts in a constructive manner.

Emotional intelligence is crucial in both personal and professional settings. It contributes to better teamwork, leadership, and adaptability in rapidly changing environments.

Self-awareness of Emotions: Recognizing your own emotions is the first step in emotional intelligence. When you understand how you feel, you're better equipped to manage your emotions and make informed decisions. This self-awareness allows you to respond to situations with emotional balance.

Empathy: Empathy, a critical component of emotional intelligence, is the ability to understand and share the feelings of others. It allows you to connect on a deeper level with people, show compassion, and offer support when needed. Empathetic individuals are skilled at recognizing the emotions of others and responding in a sensitive and appropriate manner.

Effective Communication: Emotional intelligence enhances communication skills. When you are aware of your own emotions and can interpret the emotions of others, you're better equipped to communicate your thoughts and feelings clearly and understand the perspectives of others. This fosters healthier, more constructive conversations and relationships.

Conflict Resolution: Conflict is an inevitable part of life, both personally and professionally. Emotional intelligence equips you with the tools to resolve conflicts peacefully. You can approach disagreements with understanding and empathy, seeking solutions that satisfy the needs of all parties involved.

Relationship Building: Emotional intelligence plays a crucial role in forming and maintaining strong relationships. You're better at forming meaningful connections, earning trust, and creating a supportive network of friends, colleagues, and mentors.

Leadership: Effective leaders often possess high levels of emotional intelligence. They can inspire and motivate their teams, understand their team members' needs and concerns, and make decisions that consider both the emotional and practical aspects of a situation.

Teamwork: In both personal and professional settings, effective teamwork is essential. Emotional intelligence contributes to the ability to collaborate, communicate, and resolve conflicts within a team. This leads to more productive and harmonious group dynamics.

Adaptability: In rapidly changing environments, being emotionally intelligent helps individuals and organizations adapt more effectively. Understanding and managing emotions under stress or during periods of change leads to better decision-making and problem-solving.

Well-being: High emotional intelligence is associated with greater overall well-being. Individuals with strong EQ tend to experience less stress, have more satisfying relationships, and lead more fulfilling lives.

Mindfulness:

- Mindfulness is a practice that cultivates awareness of the present moment without judgment. It involves paying attention to our thoughts, feelings, bodily sensations, and the environment.

- Mindfulness has been shown to reduce stress, increase well-being, and improve mental clarity. By being fully present in each moment, we can make more deliberate and thoughtful choices, reducing the impact of stress and anxiety.

Present-Moment Awareness: Mindfulness revolves around being fully present in the moment, without judgment. It involves paying keen attention to your thoughts, feelings, bodily sensations, and the environment around you. This practice encourages you to immerse yourself in the here and now, rather than dwelling on the past or worrying about the future.

Reducing Stress: Mindfulness has been extensively studied and found to be highly effective in reducing stress. By being present and non-judgmental, individuals can manage stressors more effectively. When you're mindful, you can observe stressful situations without becoming overwhelmed, and this often leads to more constructive responses.

Enhancing Well-Being: The practice of mindfulness has a profound impact on overall well-being. It can boost feelings of contentment, gratitude, and happiness. By focusing on the present moment, you can savor the simple joys of life and appreciate the beauty in everyday experiences.

Emotional Regulation: Mindfulness equips individuals with the tools to regulate their emotions. By acknowledging and accepting their feelings without judgment, they can better understand and control their emotional responses. This leads to improved emotional intelligence and healthier interactions with others.

Mental Clarity and Focus: Mindfulness enhances mental clarity and concentration. When you practice mindfulness, you're better able to direct your attention to the task at hand. This has a positive impact on productivity and problem-solving abilities.

Reducing Anxiety: One of the significant benefits of mindfulness is its capacity to reduce anxiety. By grounding yourself in the present, you can prevent anxious thoughts about the future from taking over. This practice can help individuals break the cycle of worrying and reduce symptoms of anxiety disorders.

Enhancing Relationships:** Mindfulness also plays a role in improving relationships. When you're fully present with someone, you listen more attentively, express empathy, and offer genuine support. This fosters healthier, more meaningful connections with others.

Mind-Body Connection: Mindfulness helps individuals become more attuned to their bodies. This can lead to better physical health as you notice signs of stress or tension and take steps to address them. It also supports a positive body image and healthier eating habits.

Personal Growth: The practice of mindfulness encourages self-reflection and personal growth. By being present and non-judgmental, individuals can more clearly identify their values and goals, ultimately leading to a more purposeful life.

4. Personal growth and development:

  - Awareness of our aspirations, values, and beliefs is essential for personal growth. When we have a clear understanding of what we want to achieve and what we stand for, we can make choices that align with our personal values and work toward our goals.

Personal growth and development are deeply intertwined with self-awareness and the conscious understanding of one's aspirations, values, and beliefs. Here's a deeper exploration of how awareness contributes to personal growth:

Clarity of Aspirations: When you are aware of your aspirations, you can set clear and meaningful goals. This clarity helps you direct your efforts toward achieving what truly matters to you, rather than aimlessly pursuing external expectations or societal norms.

Alignment with Values: Understanding your values is a cornerstone of personal growth. When you know what you stand for, you can make decisions and choices that align with your core beliefs. This alignment fosters a sense of authenticity and integrity in your actions.

Self-Discovery: Awareness of your beliefs and values often involves a process of self-discovery. As you delve deeper into your thoughts and motivations, you may uncover hidden talents, passions, and areas of interest. This self-discovery can lead to new opportunities for growth and development.

Goal Setting: Personal growth is often driven by goals. When you are aware of what you want to achieve, you can set specific, measurable, and achievable goals. This goal-setting process provides a roadmap for your personal development journey.

Overcoming Limiting Beliefs: Self-awareness enables you to identify and challenge self-limiting beliefs that hold you back. By recognizing these limiting beliefs, you can work to replace them with empowering ones that support your growth and progress.

Embracing Challenges: Personal growth involves stepping out of your comfort zone and embracing challenges. Awareness of your strengths and weaknesses can guide you in areas where you need improvement, fostering resilience and adaptability.

Emotional Intelligence: Personal growth often goes hand in hand with emotional intelligence. Understanding your own emotions and those of others enhances your interpersonal skills, empathy, and the ability to navigate complex relationships.

Adaptability: The self-awareness developed through personal growth encourages adaptability. You become more open to change, willing to learn, and capable of adjusting your approach in response to new experiences and challenges.

Resilience: Self-aware individuals tend to be more resilient in the face of setbacks. They can acknowledge their emotions, process them, and then move forward with a positive mindset. This resilience is invaluable in maintaining motivation and overcoming obstacles on the path of personal growth.

Meaning and Fulfillment: Ultimately, personal growth often leads to a greater sense of meaning and fulfillment in life. By living in accordance with your values, pursuing your aspirations, and continually learning and evolving, you can lead a more purposeful and satisfying existence.

Relationships:

Awareness plays a significant role in building and maintaining healthy relationships. Understanding the needs, desires, and boundaries of ourselves and our loved ones is essential for effective communication and conflict resolution.

Awareness is a crucial factor in building and nurturing healthy relationships, both in personal and professional contexts. Let's delve into the role of awareness in relationships and its implications:

Understanding Needs and Desires: Being aware of your own needs and desires is the first step in any relationship. When you understand what you

seek in a relationship, whether it's emotional support, companionship, or shared goals, you can communicate these needs more effectively. Similarly, recognizing the needs and desires of your loved ones is essential for meeting their expectations and fostering a fulfilling connection.
Boundaries and Respect: Awareness of boundaries is paramount in any relationship. When you're mindful of your own boundaries and those of others, you can ensure that interactions are respectful and considerate. This awareness helps prevent overstepping boundaries and maintains the mutual respect necessary for healthy relationships.

Effective Communication: Awareness enables effective communication. By being conscious of your own emotions and thoughts, you can express yourself more clearly and honestly. Furthermore, understanding the emotions and communication style of your loved ones allows you to engage in conversations that are empathetic and constructive.

Conflict Resolution: Awareness plays a critical role in conflict resolution. When conflicts arise, the ability to understand and acknowledge your own role in the situation is vital. Likewise, being aware of the perspectives and emotions of the other party helps you find common ground and resolve disagreements in a respectful manner.

Empathetic Awareness: Empathy, a deeper form of awareness, is the capacity to understand and share the feelings of others. Empathetic awareness allows you to connect on a profound level with the people in your life. You can offer emotional support, compassion, and understanding when others are going through challenges or experiencing joy.

Trust and Intimacy: Trust is built on awareness and understanding. When you're aware of the needs, boundaries, and emotions of your loved ones, trust naturally develops. Trust is a foundational element in fostering intimacy in relationships, whether they are romantic, familial, or friendship-based.

Support and Understanding: Being aware of the emotional state of your loved ones empowers you to offer support and understanding when they need it most. Whether they are going through a difficult time or celebrating an achievement, your empathetic awareness allows you to provide the right kind of support.

Strengthening Bonds: As you continue to develop awareness in your relationships, you create stronger and more resilient bonds. This strengthens the foundation of your connections, making them more enduring and fulfilling.

Personal Growth within Relationships: In relationships, awareness can lead to personal growth. When you're aware of the impact of your actions and interactions on your loved ones, you're motivated to improve and become a better partner, friend, or family member.

Personal and professional success:

In the professional realm, awareness of market trends, customer needs, and one's own strengths and weaknesses can lead to more effective decision-making and goal achievement.

Successful individuals and leaders often exhibit a high degree of awareness. They are aware of their industry, their competitors, and the ever-changing landscape of business.

Awareness is a significant contributor to personal and professional success. It equips individuals to navigate the complexities of both personal and business environments effectively. Here's a detailed look at how awareness drives success in these two realms:

Personal Success:

Self-awareness: Knowing one's own strengths, weaknesses, and aspirations is pivotal for personal success. This self-awareness allows individuals to set and pursue goals aligned with their abilities and values.

Emotional intelligence: Awareness of one's emotions and the ability to manage them is a key component of personal success. Emotionally intelligent individuals can respond to challenges, setbacks, and interpersonal situations more effectively, enhancing their overall well-being.

Clarity of goals: Being aware of one's life goals and the steps required to achieve them provides a clear roadmap for personal success. It encourages focus and determination, guiding individuals toward their desired outcomes.

Adaptability: Awareness enables individuals to adapt to changes and challenges. It helps them remain flexible in the face of unforeseen circumstances and make sound decisions to stay on track toward their goals.

Resilience: An awareness of one's limitations and the capacity to cope with adversity is essential for resilience. Resilient individuals are better equipped to bounce back from setbacks and continue their journey to personal success.

Professional Success:

Industry and market awareness: Staying informed about industry trends, market dynamics, and emerging technologies is vital for professional success. Awareness of these factors allows professionals to make informed decisions and remain competitive in their field.

Competitive intelligence: Professionals who excel in their careers are often acutely aware of their competitors. They understand their competitors' strengths and weaknesses, enabling them to strategize and position themselves more effectively.

Innovation: Awareness of emerging opportunities and potential disruptions is crucial for innovation.

Professionals who are aware of industry shifts and evolving customer needs can adapt their strategies and create innovative solutions to stay ahead.

Networking: Being aware of the value of networking and building meaningful professional relationships is essential. Networking allows individuals to leverage opportunities and gain insights from others who have achieved success.

Leadership: Successful leaders possess a high degree of awareness, both of their organization and their team. They are aware of the organizational culture, the strengths and weaknesses of their employees, and the challenges and opportunities within their industry. This awareness enables them to make informed decisions and inspire their teams effectively.

Goal setting and decision-making: In a professional context, awareness contributes to setting clear goals and making informed decisions. Professionals who understand their organization's objectives and the steps required to achieve them are more likely to make strategic decisions that lead to success.

Adaptability:

Awareness is crucial for adaptability in a rapidly changing world. Being aware of emerging technologies, global issues, and societal changes allows individuals and organizations to respond effectively and stay relevant.

Adaptability is an essential quality in a world that is constantly evolving, and awareness plays a pivotal role in enabling individuals and organizations to thrive in rapidly changing environments. Here's a closer look at the relationship between awareness and adaptability:

Awareness of Emerging Technologies: In a technologically advancing world, staying informed about new technologies and their potential applications is essential. Individuals and organizations that are aware of emerging technologies can adapt by integrating these tools to enhance productivity, efficiency, and competitiveness.

Global Issues: Awareness of global issues, such as climate change, geopolitical events, and economic trends, is crucial for adaptability. Understanding the impact of these issues on various industries and regions allows individuals and organizations to anticipate challenges and pivot when necessary.

Societal Changes: Awareness of societal changes, including shifts in demographics, consumer preferences, and cultural trends, is vital for adaptability. This awareness enables businesses to tailor their products and services to meet evolving needs and expectations.

Market Trends: Being attuned to market trends is fundamental for adaptability in business. Those who are aware of market shifts and consumer behavior can adjust their strategies and offerings to remain relevant and competitive.

Competitive Landscape: In the professional world, awareness of the competitive landscape is essential for adaptability. Knowing your competitors and understanding their strengths and weaknesses allows you to adapt your approach and remain a strong contender in your industry.

Regulatory Changes: Legislative and regulatory changes have a significant impact on businesses and industries. Awareness of impending regulations and changes in compliance requirements is critical for adaptability, as it enables organizations to make necessary adjustments to ensure compliance and sustainability.

Consumer Feedback: Being aware of customer feedback and satisfaction is vital for adaptability in providing products and services that meet their expectations. Organizations that actively seek and incorporate customer feedback can adapt to changing preferences and retain customer loyalty.

Learning and Skill Development: Personal adaptability also hinges on awareness of one's skills and the need for continuous learning and skill development. Being aware of areas where you need to grow and being open to learning new skills enhances your adaptability in a changing job market.

Environmental and Economic Factors: Awareness of environmental and economic factors, such as resource scarcity and economic trends, allows individuals and organizations to adapt by implementing sustainable practices and economic strategies that mitigate risks and seize opportunities.

Innovation: Awareness of innovation and creativity is key for adaptability. Those who actively seek new ideas, experiment, and embrace a culture of innovation are better positioned to adapt to change and create novel solutions.

Chapter 4

Entering into a discussion can be nerve-wracking, but there are several steps you can take to make the process easier:

Prepare ahead of time. If possible, research the topic beforehand and have some points or questions ready to contribute to the discussion.

Listen actively. Before you start speaking, make sure to listen actively to what others are saying. This will help you understand their perspectives and come up with relevant points to add to the conversation.

Show interest and respect. Demonstrating interest and respect for the opinions of others is a great way to build rapport and encourage open and productive discussion.

Begin with a question. Asking a question is a great way to start a discussion and can encourage others to share their thoughts.

Use open-ended questions. Avoid yes or no questions and instead, ask open-ended questions that invite people to share more information.

Be confident. Speak clearly and with conviction, and don't be afraid to share your own thoughts and ideas. Remember to keep a respectful tone, and be open to the thoughts of others.

Avoid interrupting. Interrupting can be perceived as disrespectful and can make it difficult for others to share their thoughts.

Summarize key points. Summarize key points, to ensure that everyone is on the same page and to help move the discussion forward.

Remember, entering into a discussion is about being open and engaging with others, not about being perfect or winning an argument.

CHAPTER 5

REVEALING YOUR TRUTH

Many people are depressed and unhappy with their situations, such as their jobs, where they live and most importantly, the amount of money they make. Unfortunately, in this world that we live in, money dictates who you are and your status. The more money you make, the better chance of a person you are. In addition, people tend to think this is true, to live comfortably in a world of traditions. This mindset is a false sense of reality and most of all, it's not true. You see we live in a very superficial world, which causes people to live a superficial life and not be true to who they are. Many people do not know who they are and their true value. When people live below their means, it causes them to be unhappy and depressed.

Does that sound familiar? Are you living the best life you can? Alternatively, are you living below your standards? When God created you, there is something that you single-handedly have to accomplish for you to fulfill your purpose. You may know exactly what it is or you may not quite understand what it is yet.

Living a mediocre life is not what God wants you to do. He said: "He came so we can have a life exceeding, abundantly, above all which we can ask *(**John 10:10**)*." So, if your Heavenly Father stated that in scripture then, why are you living below your standards?

You have something great inside of you, and it is important that you live the life God intended for you to live.

Unfortunately, many people are not motivated and continue living below their desired standards. Not only does living below your standards affect you, but it also affects people around you.

There is a saying, "your destiny is wrapped up in others." In this life, it is not just about you, and it's about how you make others around you better. What you do every day affects you and the people around you.

Any form of stress, depression or hurt is a tool the enemy uses to keep you down and to make you feel like you are not worth anything. It's hard to see the good side of a situation when all you feel is depressed, stressed and hurt.

People Hurt
When people are hurting, they tend to treat others the way they are feeling. When you are going through situations whether if it's good or bad, it affects those around you.

A manager of a company lived a super stressed out life. Daily she would come to work with such a nasty attitude. All the employees would talk about her ugly attitude. Little did they know, a couple of years back the manager possess good spirit until she went to the doctor and received some heart failing news. The doctor revealed to her that she was diagnosed with a tumor in her brain. The information shifted her entire outlook on life. After the manager received the news, she began to live life the best way she knew how. In this case, some people allow bad situations make them better, and other people let the unfortunate circumstances dictate their outcome. She was one! She no longer cared about others feelings. Therefore, the manager was hurting and had no problem with treating others in the same negative manner. The employees avoided her as much as possible in fear that they would be either ridiculed or written up. She had such a negative outlook on every situation that came up. The employees did not understand why she behaved in that manner until the information was exposed. Quickly the employees' shifted how they felt and started to feel sorry for their manager.

Just because an individual is hurting does not give them the right to treat others poorly. However, many people that are hurting have a pattern of doing just that.

Obstacle to Opportunity

It is better to be prepared for an opportunity and not have one than to have an opportunity and not be prepared." - Whitney Young

We all like to think life is just this fantastic walk. That nothing terrible will ever happen to us. In addition, we believe life is all peace, love, and happiness. I am not saying this cannot be true, but what I will say is before the peace, love and happiness stage you will have some monkey wrenches and hiccups along the way.

Sometimes in life we all get a hand dealt that we had no control over. We had no control over the parents we have, the family we were raised in, or the type of surrounding we grow up with. Regardless of the hand that you were dealt, the goal is to make the best of it. No matter the obstacles or situations that may occur.

Some obstacles may be big and some may be small, but no matter the size, it is a setup for an opportunity. Be prepared for an opportunity!

Do not let the hand that you were dealt, cause you not to win the game of life. Many times, in card games the person with the worst hand comes back and wins the whole game. This can be you! It will take hard work, focus, and determination, but it can be done.

One time, I met a young lady, and she had such a beautiful personality, spirit and heart. Nevertheless, I overheard people talking about her, and they judged her based on how she looked. She came from an impoverished and tough neighborhood. It is unfortunate that people will judge others without getting to know that person. The young lady knew that people judged her, but she did not allow that to stop her from being a sweet and positive person. She was determined to be someone great in life despite what others thought of her.

Don't let your past surrounding dictate where you are going in life. You have the opportunity to be, live and become the best person you desire to be.

Situations will arise and when sought through, a chance for an opportunity will show up. Do not be discouraged because of the roadblocks, or detours. It is just a setback for a setup.

When that opportunity presents itself, you need to be ready!

Do not allow fear to hold you back from being the best you. Whatever desires you have, you can achieve them. Do not let FEAR stop you from being great.

Life is too short to allow fear to cripple you and keep you from moving forward. Many people turn to drugs, alcohol or smoking to help ease the pain of fear and anxiety.

Don't be afraid of life. When you think about your situation, you start to realize that someone is in the worst situation than you. Most of the time the things that you fear is not life threatening. What is the worst that can happen?

When life can no longer threaten you with death, what else is there?

Starting that business, writing that book or speaking in front of a large crowd will not kill you. You have to step out on *Faith* and face everything and rise.

The lion may roar and growl, yet the teeth of the great lions are broken.

Too many times, I found myself in this situation. Filled with so much fear. Afraid of what people would think about me, so I lived my life in complete fear. Every time I wanted to do something, I would stop and think about what others would say, and would just talk myself out of it. To be honest, I was braver when I was a child. I was super daring, ambitious and did not care what others thought. Then, I became an adult. After becoming an adult, all of my ambition, bravery, and boldness went out the window.

All of my fears just overwhelmed me, and I was afraid to do this, I was scared to do that. Started to think to myself, "what is wrong with me?" Have to change my mindset to positive mode! "This has to come to an end," and it did.

Fear can either motivate you or cripple you. Celebrities like Jay-Z, Beyoncé and many more still have anxiety issue before going out on stage in front of millions of people. You would never know because even though they are afraid, they rise and go out on stage and give it all they got. They allowed fear to motivate them.

Fear can also be used as a blocker or building block

Fear of being diagnosed with a health scare will motivate people to lose weight. They will no longer say they are big boned. I have never seen a fat skeleton... lol, have you? Others will feel sorry for themselves and hope most will feel empathy towards them.

Have you ever heard of people fearing success or being Wealthy? It sounds crazy, but many people suffer from the overwhelming feeling of success.

Think about babies taking their first steps. In the beginning, they may be a little afraid, but they keep trying. No matter how many times they fall or get hurt, they keep working until they get it right. Babies do not allow anything or anyone to stop them from taking their first steps. They get back up and keep trying until they succeed.

Fear can motivate you... Diagnosis will make people get their health in order; such as lose weight/ big boned or not. Remember that fat skeleton. LOL

Yes, life happens, obstacles may come, things may not go the way you planned; however, you have to continue to push through to get what you want out of life.

Do Not Let Regret & Fear Replace Your Dreams
I should have,

I could have,
I would have,
However, I did not.

In actuality, if you want to do something **JUST DO IT***!* In addition, I know, it is easier said than done, but it is just that simple.

Regret will only bring you down and make you feel like you are a failure.

People are always quick to tell you, what you are not doing and what you need to do. Instead of telling you, what they like about what you did. It is your job to encourage yourself and be content with the decisions that you make.

If you do not like the decisions that you have made, change them. Start owning your decisions and making sure that you are happy with the future choices that you make. It is your life, and it is time to take ownership of it.

Your dreams and goals are super important to you. Do not let false evidence appearing real; stop you from accomplishing your dreams and goals.

You can achieve your goals and dream. Here is a scripture:

I can do all things through Christ who gives me strength.
The Lord is with you at all time. Even when you feel weak, He is there. He will give you what you need to get you to where you need to go. God knows the desire of your heart; He wants you to give it to him. Every hurt, pain or weakness, God is waiting with open arms to help you. You can do it.

If you want to start that business, do it! If you are going to write that book, do it! If you are going to go for that promotion, go for it! Face Everything and Rise. You can do it!

What would your life be like if you did not allow your fear to creep in and stop you? What would your future look like?

Take a moment, close your eyes and meditate... What does it look and feel like to set out and accomplish your goals, eliminating FEAR?

Stop Procrastinating
A study shows that 20% of people consider themselves as chronic procrastinators. Procrastination is the lack of self-motivation. It is the route to killing your dreams and goals.

A man named Bill decided that he was going to stop allowing procrastinating to defeat him and decided to buy a book called 50 Steps to Defeating Procrastination. It has been a little over ten years, and he still is trying to schedule a time to read the book.

Do not be like Bill. When you put your mind to something, get it done. Procrastination is the thief of time.

Back in college, I can remember my professor giving the class a paper due the following week. Being the kind of college student that will wait until the night before and pull an all-nighter because of direct procrastination.
Unfortunately, this behavior has spilled over into real life and procrastination have become the killer of many people dreams and goals.

Time is valuable, important and you can never get it back. Prioritizing your goals and get them done.

Waiting until the time is right or when you get that time from your busy schedule to do something may take forever to get there. You will be waiting all of your life to complete something that can change your life if you will only stop procrastinating.

Stop letting Social Media control your day. Social Media is another form of procrastination. So many people spend numerous hours on social media. Such as spending 2 hours a day, 14 hours a week and averaging about 56 hours a month just scrolling and watching others live a fake life is not productive. If you spent 56 hours focusing on your dreams and goals, you would be successful in achieving your dreams.

Another essential tool to stop procrastination is writing a daily to-do list. This can help you prioritize your day. However, if you are writing the same to do list every day and not completing the task at hand, you will be procrastinating. When you make your daily to-do list be sure to achieve as much as possible, starting with the most important task moving to the less important task. Do not leave the hard task for last. Do it first, then everything after that will be a breeze.

If you continue to put your to-do list off, it will continue to grow and will make you feel overwhelmed and unaccomplished. You have the willpower to complete whatever it is that you put your mind to.

Stop Being Basic

If God created you in His image, why do you live below your value?

I am not just talking about spending money on yourselves to feel good. I am talking about living like royalty, feeling like royalty and acting like royalty.

If you are a Child of the Most High, you have inherited what your heavenly *Father* has. You should live and treat yourself as such.

Also, if you lived how God sees you, it will eliminate stress and depression. You have to believe that you are amazing and worth living an amazing and incredible life. Being basic should not be in your vocabulary. You are royalty and if you believe that, now is the time to start speaking, acting and living like royalty.

If you were a King or a Queen, would you act the way you currently act?

Would you dress the way you currently dress?
Would you entertain the people that are currently in your life?
Would you put up with the things you currently put up with?

For instance, I asked my son, "Why were you misbehaving at school today?" he said, "I don't know! Mommy" and in return, I said, "What if we as a family found out that Mommy was a daughter of the Emperor of a country?"

"How would you feel?" He said, "Oh Mommy, I will be super excited!"

I said, "will you tell anyone?" and he said, "Yes, mommy I will tell everyone!" Then I asked him, "How would you act?"

Then he said, " I will walk around with my head up high, and when I get to class, I will sit down in my chair slow so everyone can see me," I laughed and said, "Okay, how will you acted inside of the class?"

He said," I will act like the boss." I said and "how does a boss act?" He said, very stern and focused".

I responded exactly! So just to let you know mommy is a daughter of a King, which means you are a grandson of a king, He says, "huh" Is grandpa a King? I said, No, Jesus Christ is the King of all Kings, so this point forward I need you to act like royalty that you are"!

A quick lesson learned that you need to stop being basic or not valuing yourselves and take more pride in who you are and whose you are.

Only the Strong Will Survive- Stop Being Weak

Being weak and trying to survive in this life will not work. In this life, we all have heard that this life will chew you up and spit you out.
Just like the story of David and Goliath. Even though Goliath was strong and supposedly David was weak, it was David who had the spirit of God on his side.

Actuality David was strong spiritually. So let me explain, when I say the strong will survive I'm talking about strong spiritually and not physically. All of our battles are physical which stems from the spiritual world. Learning how to strengthen your spiritual life through reading God's word and prayer will help you conquer many battles.

Chapter 6

Understanding Confidence and Self-Esteem

In the vast tapestry of human emotions and experiences, few threads are as integral to our well-being and success as confidence and self-esteem. As we embark on this journey to master these essential attributes, we must first lay the foundation by delving into their true essence, exploring their impact, and learning to distinguish healthy self-perception from its less benevolent counterparts.

Defining Confidence and Self-Esteem

Confidence is more than mere bravado or an outward display of self-assuredness. It's the internal assurance that fuels our actions, the belief that we possess the skills and competence to face challenges head-on. It's an intrinsic sense of self-reliance that allows us to navigate life's twists and turns with resilience.

Self-esteem, on the other hand, is the bedrock upon which confidence is built. It's the deeply rooted perception of our own worthiness and value. When we possess a healthy self-esteem, we acknowledge our imperfections while recognizing our unique strengths and contributions. It acts as a buffer against the storms of self-doubt, shielding us from the corrosive effects of negativity.

The Impact of Low Confidence and Self-Esteem

Imagine the heavy burden of walking through life with shrouded self-doubt and a persistent lack of belief in your abilities. Low confidence and self-esteem cast a shadow over every endeavor, leading to missed opportunities, unfulfilled potential, and a life constrained by fear. Individuals grappling with these challenges often find themselves held back by internal barriers that hinder progress and stifle growth.

The effects extend far beyond the individual, echoing into relationships, career choices, and overall well-being. Low confidence can inhibit effective communication, hinder decision-making, and deter one from pursuing their passions. The resulting cycle of missed chances and self-fulfilling prophecies reinforces the negative self-image, creating a self-perpetuating loop of self-doubt.

Recognizing the Signs of Healthy and Unhealthy Self-Image

Distinguishing between a healthy and an unhealthy self-image is a crucial step on the path to mastery. A healthy self-image is characterized by an accurate perception of strengths and weaknesses, the ability to acknowledge areas for growth without devaluing oneself, and a sense of self-assuredness that isn't contingent on external validation.

In contrast, an unhealthy self-image often manifests as excessive self-criticism, a constant need for validation, and a habit of comparing oneself unfavorably to others. These negative patterns not only erode confidence and self-esteem but also contribute to anxiety, stress, and even mental health issues.

As we traverse the landscape of this book, we will delve deeper into these concepts, unraveling the threads of confidence and self-esteem to better understand their nuances and how they intertwine. Through self-reflection, practical exercises, and insightful guidance, you will equip yourself with the tools to reshape your self-perception and forge a path toward unwavering self-belief.

Remember, the journey to mastering confidence and self-esteem is not about becoming a different person, but rather about uncovering and nurturing the essence of who you already are. With each turning page, you're setting foot on a transformative path that holds the promise of greater self-awareness, empowerment, and a future rich with belief in yourself.

Chapter 7

Embrace Self-Acceptance

Embracing Authenticity:

True self-acceptance begins with embracing your authentic self. It means acknowledging that you are a unique individual with a distinct set of qualities, talents, and characteristics that make you who you are. Embrace your true self and let go of the need to conform to societal expectations or seek external validation.

Recognizing Strengths:

Self-acceptance involves recognizing and appreciating your strengths. Take time to identify your natural talents, skills, and abilities. Celebrate your achievements and acknowledge the value you bring to the world. Embracing your strengths allows you to build confidence and reinforces your belief in your capabilities.

Embracing Imperfections:
Nobody is perfect, and self-acceptance requires embracing your imperfections. Accept that you have weaknesses and areas where you may fall short. Rather than dwelling on them, view them as opportunities for growth and learning. Embracing imperfections with kindness and compassion allows you to cultivate self-acceptance and self-belief.

Letting Go of Comparison:
Comparison is the thief of joy and a barrier to self-acceptance. When we constantly compare ourselves to others, we diminish our self-worth and undermine our belief in ourselves. Let go of the need to measure up to others and focus on your own journey. Recognize that everyone has

their own unique path and that your worth is not determined by how you stack up against others.

Practicing Self-Compassion:

Self-acceptance involves treating yourself with kindness and compassion. Cultivate a gentle and understanding attitude towards yourself, especially during challenging times. Acknowledge that making mistakes is part of being human and offer yourself forgiveness and understanding. Self-compassion allows you to develop a healthy relationship with yourself and fosters self-belief.

Accepting Limitations:

Self-acceptance means accepting your limitations. We all have areas where we may struggle or face limitations. Rather than viewing them as weaknesses, recognize them as areas for growth and seek support or alternative strategies when needed. Embracing your limitations with grace and self-compassion allows you to navigate challenges with confidence and resilience.

Challenging Negative Self-Talk:
Negative self-talk can erode self-acceptance and self-belief. Become aware of your inner dialogue and challenge negative thoughts and self-criticism. Replace them with positive affirmations and supportive self-talk. Cultivate a mindset that encourages self-acceptance and reinforces your belief in your abilities.

Embracing Personal Growth:
Self-acceptance is not a stagnant state but a continuous journey of personal growth. Embrace opportunities for self-improvement and expansion. Engage in activities that nourish your mind, body, and soul. Pursue hobbies, learn new skills, and seek knowledge. Embracing personal growth supports self-acceptance by allowing you to discover and develop your potential.

Chapter 8

Best Version Of Yourself

Being the best version of yourself is the most important aspect of your life to master. It's having the ability to breakthrough what's holding you back and really living a life that inspires other people. It's all about controlling your state of mind especially when life gets tough and you're in a rut.

Controlling your state is by far the most important key to manifesting any success because if something happens that we can't control, it's up to you to control your state in those moments. An emotional state is a feeling for example we are either happy, excited, passionate, depressed, frustrated or overwhelmed.

These are all states. Going from stressed to excited is easy, going from depressed to feeling grateful is easy. All you need to know is how to trigger these emotions off at will and it all starts with what controls your emotional state. Your body controls your state whether your happy today or sad today is a reflection of where you are holding your body. If someone is depressed where are they holding their body? Everything would we down, slouched and they would hardly be breathing so that's controlling everything.

If you look at someone who is excited, their body is looking completely different to someone whose depressed. Everything's up, moving rapidly, moving freely and they are smiling consistently. Every emotion we feel is a pattern. It's a pattern of the way we use our body and a pattern about what we tend to focus on.

Realize that you are in control of your mind and you can feel whatever you want to feel right now. Most people conditioned themselves to feel depressed everyday but you have the ability to feel happy everyday.

Clients of mine say to me, 'I just want to experience freedom, if I went on a holiday to the other side of the world, all my problems would disappear.' The truth is that's not going to do anything but give you a different experience of life for the moment. It's like putting a bandaid over a cut. If you haven't dealt with the source of the problem up front, then it will always be there.

A guy I talked to today told me he just wanted to feel free; My simple answer back was, 'just be free now.' He said, 'I can't be free now, I have too much responsibility.' Look at the story he is telling himself, he is postponing his freedom because he tells himself a BS story which is holding him back from feeling free.

Start being conscious of the stories you tell yourself because that's what I am waiting for with every client I see. Whether it's someone saying 'I don't have the time,' or 'I'm big boned' all these are stories that we tell ourselves that keep us comfortable in the moment. I know for a fact that there is someone out there in this world that is busier than you but still finds the time to do certain things and why they find the time is because it's important to them. We only find time to do things that are important to us and it takes people a long time to make exercise or spending time with their partner important.

The only reason you don't have what you want is because you have a story about why you can't have it. So you need to be conscious of the stories you're telling yourself and once you have awareness then you have the power to change it.

Write down exactly what you want to create in your life, your biggest goal and then ask yourself this question, why can't I have that goal now, what's holding me back from manifesting that goal?

By you doing this you are going to find out the stories and beliefs that are holding you back and that's what you must find out. We can then use techniques that will clear what's holding you back.

So once you have a written down all the beliefs and stories, you are going to do a process called limiting belief clearing and this will clear that belief. First step is before we start; You must want to change and that's half the battle. If you really want to see massive change throughout this book, make it a must to do these techniques.

CLEARING LIMITING BELIEFS

1. Write down all the limiting beliefs that are not serving you.
2. Once you've done this, pick one at a time. The most effective way to clear this once and for all is to get your brain to associate massive immediate pain to this belief. You must feel deep in your gut that not only has this belief cost you pain in your past, but it's costing you pain in the present and ultimately, can bring you pain in your future.
3. After you have associated immediate pain to that belief, your brain will be in the position to do anything to change so then you must associate tremendous pleasure to adopting a new empowering belief to take its place.

4. Remember, if you clear your limiting beliefs, your life will free up more than anything you do. Remember that it's really important to actually feel the pain for a short five to ten minutes and do whatever it takes. The short period of pain for a lifetime of freedom is worth it.

Chapter 9

Impact on Well-Being:

This section sheds light on how this complex affects mental and emotional health, highlighting the importance of addressing it. Let's delve deeper into the impact on well-being:

Anxiety: Feelings of inadequacy and self-doubt are often at the root of anxiety. An inferiority complex can lead to excessive worry and a constant fear of failure. This chronic state of unease can manifest in various forms of anxiety disorders, such as generalized anxiety disorder or social anxiety, ultimately compromising one's overall mental well-being.

Depression: An inferiority complex can be a significant contributor to depression. The persistent feelings of not measuring up, self-loathing, and a lack of self-worth can lead to a profound sense of hopelessness and sadness.

Individuals may become trapped in a cycle of negativity and self-criticism, negatively impacting their emotional health.

Low Self-Esteem: Low self-esteem is a direct consequence of an inferiority complex. It can erode an individual's confidence and self-worth, leading to a negative self-image. Low self-esteem affects how one perceives themselves and how they interact with the world. It can limit their aspirations and hinder personal growth.

Relationship Strain: An inferiority complex can have a ripple effect on personal relationships. People who feel inadequate may struggle with trust, communication, and intimacy. It can lead to social withdrawal, difficulty in forming connections, and even strained family relationships. The complex can act as a barrier to healthy and fulfilling relationships, further impacting one's well-being.

Physical Health: The psychological distress caused by an inferiority complex can manifest physically. Chronic stress, which often accompanies this complex, can lead to a range of health issues, including high blood pressure, sleep disturbances, and a compromised immune system. Thus, the impact is not limited to mental well-being; it can affect physical health as well.

Missed Opportunities: An inferiority complex can prevent individuals from seizing opportunities for personal and professional growth. Fear of failure and a belief in one's inadequacy can lead to avoidance behaviors, causing missed chances for development and success. These missed opportunities can, in turn, negatively impact overall life satisfaction.

VII. Emotional Resilience: People with an inferiority complex may struggle with emotional resilience. They may find it challenging to bounce back from setbacks, as their belief in their inadequacy reinforces negative self-talk and self-criticism. A lack of emotional resilience can hinder one's ability to cope with life's challenges.

Chapter 10

How to Identify Your Positive Qualities and Gain a More Objective View of Yourself

You know how unhealthy a negative self-image can be. And really, when your self-beliefs are incorrectly critical, you are cheating yourself of a happy and successful existence. The last couple of sections you learned exactly what low self-esteem is, how to identify its symptoms, and how to challenge unhealthy beliefs that are not factual.

But if you suffer from LSE, that may sound a lot easier than it actually is. Years of problematic thinking and cognitive distortion can probably not be changed overnight. After all, even if you identify incorrect beliefs that you have about yourself, and you begin to question and challenge them, you may still suffer thoughts of inadequacy and failure.

This means you need to begin to identify your positive qualities. Then, whenever limiting self-beliefs begin to appear, you can remind yourself that your negative self-thoughts are obviously incorrect, since you have these outstanding characteristics and habits.

You can do this with a simple list. On a piece of paper, write down 5 things you like about yourself. Don't think about anything negative. Think about successes you have had in your life, good relationships, memorable occasions and events. If you find yourself writing down more than 5 positive self-beliefs, excellent!

Another way to identify your positive qualities is to study the following list. These are words that psychologists have identified as evidence of positive self-beliefs and behaviors:

- Friendly
- Generous
- Grateful
- Loyal
- Patient
- Persistent
- Punctual
- Respectful
- Sensitive
- Sincere
- Alert
- Compassionate
- Confident
- Cooperative
- Courteous
- Creative
- Decisive
- Disciplined
- Discrete

- Enthusiastic
- Forgiving

Now think about what types of behaviors you exhibit that qualify you for those descriptive terms. A person with LSE may be cooperative, generous and always on time. However, because of limiting self-thoughts, they do not notice that these are awesome, positive qualities.

But that is exactly what they are! Another way to identify positive character traits is to simply type "Positive Personality Adjectives" into an Internet search engine. This will give you a list of things to look for in your life that help you recognize when your self-limiting negative self-image is incorrect.

Do not get too full of yourself, though. Remember, an abnormally high self-image can be just as harmful as a low self-image. So, how do you develop a more realistic and objective view of yourself? By always viewing your successes and failures, achievements and mistakes with a grain of salt.

You can do that by stepping outside of your situation. Look at your behaviors, beliefs and thoughts from a logical and analytical point of view. This needs to be an unemotional, straightforward, honest appraisal. However, you must be neutral as well. Look at both sides of the possible situation, action or thought process.

Remember that human beings will make mistakes, you and everyone else. Grade your mental believes and actions with a *"reality measuring stick"* rather than an emotional one. Recognize and embrace your failures, do not ignore them, but do not overstate them either.

Finding honest friends is a great way to keep yourself grounded, and listen to criticism only from those people that you know will speak to you truthfully. It can be tough to develop an objective view of your beliefs and actions, and it all begins with being honest with yourself.

Chapter 11

Meeting someone for the first time can be nerve-wracking, but there are several steps you can take to make the process easier:

Smile and make eye contact. Smile and make eye contact when you first meet someone. This shows that you're friendly and approachable.

Introduce yourself. Give your name, and ask for their name.

Break the ice. Ask them a question or make a comment about your surroundings, such as the weather, or event you are attending.

Show interest. Ask them about themselves, their work or family. Show genuine interest in getting to know them.

Listen actively. Pay attention to what they have to say, and respond thoughtfully.

Be yourself. Be true to who you are, and don't try to be someone you're not.

Use open-ended questions. Avoid yes or no questions and instead, ask open-ended questions that invite people to share more information.

End the conversation gracefully. If the conversation comes to a natural end, thank the person for their time and exchange contact information if appropriate.

Remember, talking to someone for the first time is about building a connection, not about impressing them. Be friendly, open, and genuine, and you'll be more likely to make a good first impression.

Chapter 12

Health and everything else.

Are you happy with what you have Co-created?

Do you want a change?

I remember the first time I realized that I co-created my life, I was torn. I couldn't believe it. Being so unhappy, lonely, broke, overweight, lived in a horrible neighborhood and just miserable.
Hated my job and disliked my co-workers.
Thinking to myself, there's no way I could love myself by allowing my situation to get the best of me.
I didn't know any better. Nobody never taught this to me. I told myself I had to do better. I started reading books, listening to audios, watching video on how to improve my mindset

and my life. Many years later, here I am sharing this gift with you.

It may seem like a lot in the beginning, but I will assure you that it will be all worth it in the end. One of the things that got me going is repetition.

I had to do things that others won't, to live the life that others don't.

I stop listening to senseless gestures and started to see my eyes and ears as a gateway. I started to realize how powerful words can be when spoken into the atmosphere. I became more alert and careful about what I spoke out of my mouth.

Affirmations

The action or process of affirming something or being affirmed.

When was the last time you affirmed something?

Affirming something in your lives may seem difficult, but it's not.

"Sticks and stones may break my bones but words will never hurt me"~ Anonymous

If you are anything like me, as much as this sounds great, we both know that words can hurt you.

People will always have something negative to say to stop you from feeling great or moving towards your destination. They will always identify all of your flaws. You must not indulge in negative conversation or small talk because remember whatever you speak into the atmosphere will most likely manifest. Be careful! When was the last time you said something good about yourself?

If people constantly speak negative, who is going behind them and reversing every ill spoken word over their life.

One day I was mentoring a group of middle school kids and we started talking about Affirmations. I explained to them how powerful words are. I showed the following *Exercise*

Bowl Exercise
Reflects all the *negative* things that people have said about them.
All the negative things! What their mom, dad, teacher, friend, and anyone else we thought of had that have said anything negative about them. There was a bowl with balls and the balls represented negative words. As you already know, this bowl was overflowing with about 25 balls.
Reflects all the *positive* things that people have said about them
All the positive things! Compliments, encouragement and nice things of what mom, dad, teacher, friends and anyone else we could

have thought of. In this bowl, there was about 3-4 balls representing the number of positive words.

These kids were shocked. If we are co-creators like we discussed earlier, then why do we allow others to create our world? We allow others to speak things over our lives when we have the power to speak things into our own lives as many times a day as possible.

After the bowl exercise...............

When you first start with your Affirmation it may feel funny especially if you have never done it before. As you continue to do it, it will start to unveil the power of your words.

Look into who you are and what you want to be and start speaking these things over your life.

Create a list. List all the things that you desire to be and what you think of yourself.

List-

AM Beautiful - you may not currently feel like you are beautiful but this is a desire of where you want to be or feel.

If you're not the great of a cook... Your List should say.

AM a great cook

These are just examples of how you will create your list of positive words that you will like to establish in your life.

Now, make your List….. Here's an example of my list when I first got started.

I AM a Best Selling Author

I AM Wealthy

I AM Healthy

I Can do All thing through Christ who strengthens me

I AM a Mighty woman of God

I AM an Amazing mother

I AM an Incredible wife

I AM the head and not the tail

I AM above and not beneath

During this exercise, DO NOT listen to anyone else thoughts about you. This list needs to reflect what you think about you, what God says about you and where you desire to be. Stop looking for others Approval. Only approval you need is God! After establishing your list, if we were to go back to the bowl exercise, the negative words others have spoken over your life that was in bowl 1 and bowl 2 had the positive words, would it made a difference? How do you think it will play out? After Affirming who you are and whose you are, you will become those examples and things will look a little different.

Bowl Exercise 2

Bowl 1

Negative words that was about to overflow.

Bowl 2

Positive words... I AM....

We don't have to wait on others to provide us with positive words because we speak positivity over our own life..... and fill up the bowl with positive words.

Your affirmation needs to be established every day and repeated daily.

Repetition is powerful! Doing it first thing in the morning will start to reflect in your subconscious mind.

Why daily? Because every day it should be your desire to create a better life for yourself.

Affirming who you are on a daily basis will cancel out all the negative words that others may have spoken or even have thought in their minds about you.

Reap What You Sow

What are you sowing? You may have heard this saying so many times, but no one discusses what

they are sowing. Everyone wants to reap the benefits but don't want to put in the work.
Putting in the work is how you will reap, whether it's, praying and fasting to gain a deeper connection with God, or working out and eating healthy to live a healthier life
Sowing reminds me of Karma. What you put out is what you will get in return!
Everyone wants to live an amazing wealthy lifestyle with all the money, cars and mansion. However, when individuals see the amount of sowing/work those individuals put in they no longer want that lifestyle anymore because it's a lot of work.
What have you sown?
It's just as simple as giving back, whether it's paying tithes, blessing others that are less fortunate or giving to a charity.
Every big corporation have a charity that they give back to whether they believe in God or not.

Giving back is another *law of the land*. You will reap whether you are a Christian or not. This is something that has been established before Christianity was formed.

When was the last time you gave?

People have a tendency to not give. When they get their pay they want to hold onto it and the key to prosperity is you have to give a portion back.

This is a necessity if you what to reap. You have to sow a seed in order for that seed to grow so it can bear fruit.

Many people don't want to sow, but they want to reap a harvest. That's like you going over to a seed that was never placed into the soil, water it and waiting for it to flourish. How will it flourish if you have never sown a seed? It will never grow because the seed was never placed in soil to grow.

This may be a hard pill to swallow; however, this is important and if we don't *give,* as the bible says, we are robbing God.

Will a man rob God? Yet you are robbing me. But you say, 'How have we robbed you?' In your tithes and contributions.

Yes, it is possible that we can rob God by not giving our tithes and offering.

In All Things See the Good

If you were to look at your surroundings, you will be able to notice so many things that you don't like. I want you to take that same look around and start thinking about all the things you do like.

It's time now to stop focusing on all the negative that surrounds you and start paying attention to all of the positive. In all things, see the good.

See good in people, situation and every obstacle that comes up.

Some people are programmed to think objectively. "Oh no, what now"? Or, what's the worst that can happen?
Instead of them saying, "Lord, why me", began to saying "Thank You God. It could've been worst." People need to let go of the negative state of mind and start recognizing that someone out there is in a worst situation than them. Be grateful!

Start enjoying the people and things that are around you. Start looking at things differently. When you wake up, take a moment, smell the roses, enjoy where you are in life and who you are in life.
No, you may not be where you want to be, but you're not where you use to be and remember the best is yet to come.
Be grateful for the little things.

Live Life to the Fullest

This is your life. No one else can live it for you. Every day you wake up, God has given you another chance to be great and to chase your dreams. Stop taking life for granted. People are dying every day and before you leave this earth, you need to make the best of your situation.

Stop looking for others to make you happy. Happiness starts from within. Only you can truly make you happy.

Start living your life, how you want it to be. Do something different each day.

- Take a different route to work
- Get a membership at a gym
- Try a new restaurant
- Go to networking events
- Meet new people
- Start listening to music
- Plan a date with your spouse, if you haven't gone out in a while

- Change your hair
- Wear something different.

Get out of that boring cycle of things and start to change your routine.

You have to do something different to get a different outcome. Life is too short to be old and miserable. Enjoy the moment and everyone around you.

Start smiling and embracing the person that God has created, which is YOU!

Chapter 13

How to Start Your Morning

The way you start your morning have an effect on the rest of your day. Starting your morning right will set the tone for the rest of your day.

The *power hour* is the first hour of the morning which is also the most powerful hour of your day. Most people morning start off rough. Their alarm will go off, and they make the decision to go back to sleep and get a little more rest. When they do decide to wake up, they're now running late. They spent their morning running around trying to gather all that they need for work. When they finally get on the road, they are utterly driving like a maniac. Everyone else is driving the speed limit and they're the only one in a rush. Now, they get to work a couple of minutes late and forgot they had an important meeting in the morning with the executive boss.

That scenario sounds like a lot of people I know. The art of being on time says a lot about an individual.

Taking control of your morning starts with you getting a good night's rest. Going to bed 4 am and waking up 6 am is not the ideal rest that your body needs.

Go to bed on time. Give yourself time to rest and allow your body to recover from a day's work.

This power hour can be changed to fit your schedule. Customize it and make it your own.

The three primary focus is your **mind, body**, and **spirit**. These are the three things that people are always trying to better. But one needs the other. Just increasing your body and not your mind is a waste. Here are the keys to starting your morning:

Power Hour keeps you motivated!

The first 20 minutes consist of prayer, spending time with God. Telling God thank you for waking you up in the morning and focusing on the things you are grateful for. The attitude of gratitude, spending time seeing yourself being that amazing person you want to be, and spending a moment to reflect on how you will feel if you were living that amazing life that you desire.

The second 20 minutes consist of reading, empowering and educating your mind. This may be spent by you reading the bible, a book that will help increase areas in your life that you will like to work on or an audio that you will listen to that will help motivate and inspire you. This will help stimulate your mind and get you ready to start your day.

The last 20 minutes will consist of you working out or doing some form of a physical activity. You can go for a walk or do something that will get your blood flowing. This one is important because you will get your physical work out and get your energy level increased. This will be a light form of physical activity to clear your mind and get you ready to start your day.

Once your power hour is completed, you may begin your day.

You Are, What You Say

Whatever you say, is usually a reflection of who you are. When was the last time you said something positive about yourself?

People that have self-doubt normally has low self-esteem. People who speak highly of themselves normally are confident individuals.

You have to get to the place in your life where you stop speaking as though you are disguised with who you are and start taking pride in yourself.

What are you saying about yourself?

Speak Life into Yourself

Speaking life into yourself is key to self-love. Stop waiting on others to tell you and start telling yourself. You are amazing and you can do it!
You have to start looking in the mirror and start speaking to that person that you see.
If you had an opportunity to tell the younger you what to do, what will you tell the younger you?
If you're visited by a more attractive, vibrant, successful and confident version of you, a version of who you desired to be. What would they want to tell you?
Everything is going to be okay! You can do it! Don't be afraid! You have to get in the habit of speaking life into yourself, meaning speaking great thing to yourself. It's okay to speak to yourself. You are beautiful and amazing and never forget that

Chapter 14

The Mindset of Confidence

Embracing a Growth Mindset

Imagine your mind as a garden, and your thoughts as the seeds you plant. A growth mindset is the nurturing soil that allows those seeds to flourish. When you embrace a growth mindset, you understand that your abilities and intelligence are not fixed, but rather can be developed through effort, learning, and perseverance. This mindset empowers you to see challenges as opportunities for growth, setbacks as stepping stones, and failures as lessons on the path to mastery.

Overcoming Limiting Beliefs and Self-Doubt

We all carry with us a mental attic filled with beliefs that have accumulated over the years. Some beliefs lift us up, while others weigh us down with self-doubt and limitations. These limiting beliefs often emerge from past experiences, societal expectations, or the opinions of others. In this section, you'll learn to shine a light on these beliefs, question their validity, and replace them with affirmations that reinforce your self-worth and potential.

Cultivating Positive Self-Talk and Inner Dialogue

Your thoughts are a constant stream of chatter, an inner dialogue that profoundly influences your perception of yourself and the world around you. The power of this dialogue cannot be understated – it can either be a source of encouragement or a wellspring of self-sabotage. By cultivating positive self-talk, you create an atmosphere of self-encouragement and self-compassion. You'll explore techniques to challenge negative self-talk and replace it with affirmations that empower and uplift.

Remember, your mind is a powerful tool, and how you wield it shapes your reality. The good news is that just as you can train your body to become stronger, you can train your mind to become more resilient, confident, and positive. As you journey through this chapter, engage in self-reflection, embrace new practices, and open yourself to the transformative potential of a mindset that believes in your abilities and worth. The seeds you plant today will bloom into the confident future you aspire to create.

Chapter 15

Cultivate Positive Self-Talk

Understanding the Power of Self-Talk:

Self-talk refers to the ongoing internal dialogue we have with ourselves. It shapes our thoughts, emotions, and actions, influencing our self-perception and overall mindset. Recognize that the way we talk to ourselves has a direct impact on our self-belief and confidence. By understanding the power of self-talk, we can harness it as a tool for personal growth and empowerment.

Identifying Negative Self-Talk:

Begin by identifying negative self-talk patterns. Notice the critical or self-defeating thoughts that arise in different situations. Pay attention to the language and tone you use when speaking to yourself. Common examples of negative self-talk include self-doubt, self-blame, and harsh self-criticism. Awareness is the first step in transforming negative self-talk into positive and constructive inner dialogue.

Challenging Negative Self-Talk:

Challenge negative self-talk by questioning its validity and accuracy. Ask yourself if there is evidence to support these negative thoughts. Often, negative self-talk is rooted in limiting beliefs or distorted perceptions. Replace self-criticism with self-compassion and understanding. Treat yourself with the same kindness and encouragement you would offer a friend. By challenging negative self-talk, you create space for positive self-encouragement to thrive.

Practicing Positive Affirmations:

Positive affirmations are powerful statements that reinforce positive self-beliefs and qualities. Create a list of affirmations that resonate with you and align with your goals and values. Repeat these affirmations regularly, both in your mind and out loud. Choose affirmations that promote self-belief, resilience, and empowerment. By practicing positive affirmations, you rewire your self-talk to be uplifting and supportive.

Using Constructive Inner Dialogue:

Develop constructive inner dialogue that encourages growth and self-empowerment. Instead of dwelling on mistakes or shortcomings, focus on lessons learned and areas for improvement. Replace self-defeating statements with constructive questions and statements that foster problem-solving and growth. Engage in a dialogue that nurtures self-belief, resilience, and a solution-oriented mindset.

Seeking and Accepting Compliments:

Acknowledge and accept compliments graciously. Often, we tend to downplay or dismiss compliments, which perpetuates negative self-talk. Instead, internalize compliments and use them as evidence of our strengths and capabilities. Embrace positive feedback as validation of our efforts and accomplishments. By seeking and accepting compliments, we reinforce positive self-talk and bolster our self-belief.

Surrounding Yourself with Positivity:

Create an environment that fosters positive self-talk. Surround yourself with supportive and uplifting individuals who believe in your abilities and encourage your personal growth. Engage in activities and hobbies that bring joy and positivity into your life. Limit exposure to negative influences, whether it be people, media, or self-comparisons.

www.ingramcontent.com/pod-product-compliance
Lightning Source LLC
LaVergne TN
LVHW010222070526
838199LV00062B/4685